SPIDERFLY

by John Webber

Spiderfly was first performed at Theatre503, London,
on 6 November 2019.

SPIDERFLY

by John Webber

Cast

ESTHER	**Lia Burge**
CHRIS / KEITH	**Matt Whitchurch**

Creative Team

Director:	**Kirsty Patrick Ward**
Set & Costume Design	**Lizzy Leech**
Lighting Design	**Peter Small**
Sound Design	**Dominic Brennan**
Stage Manager	**Rose Hockaday**
Assistant Director	**Lucy Grace McCann**
Casting Director	**Christopher Worrall**

Spiderfly was first produced by **Sofi Berenger** & **George Warren** for **Metal Rabbit Productions** in association with **Theatre503** in November 2019

Assistant Producer	**Oliver Seymour**
Assistant Producer (Marketing)	**Andre Sequeira**

BIOGRAPHIES

LIA BURGE (ESTHER)

Lia trained at LAMDA. Theatre credits include: *I Know My Husband Loves Me* (Union Theatre;) *Lady in the Van* (Theatre Royal Bath); *Romeo and Juliet* (Orange Tree Theatre); *Freak* (Theatre503); *The Taming of the Shrew, Macbeth, The Comedy of Errors, As You Like It, Henry IV PT 1* (Merely Theatre); *Separate Tables* (Chichester Festival Theatre). Television credits include: *EastEnders*. Lia is a Hammer&Tongue spoken word finalist and is working on several poetry projects for the page and the stage. Lia also dances the Argentine Tango and has performed in productions at Glyndebourne and Grange Park Opera.

MATT WHITCHURCH (CHRIS / KEITH)

Matt Whitchurch graduated from RADA on the BA course in 2014. His theatre credits include *A Midsummer Night's Dream* (Liverpool Everyman); *Pine, Labyrinth* (Hampstead Theatre); *The Herbal Bed* (ETT); *Pride and Prejudice* (Nottingham Playhouse) and *The Be All and End All* (York Theatre Royal). He has appeared on screen in shows such as *Call the Midwife, The Outcast, Some Girls, Casualty* (BBC) and *The Sex Pistols vs. Bill Grundy* (SKY).

KIRSTY PATRICK-WARD (DIRECTOR)

This year Kirsty will direct the world premiere of the new comedy *Groan Ups* in the West End, and will revive her hit production of Joy Wilkinson's play *The Sweet Science of Bruising* at Wilton's Music Hall. For its initial run at the Southwark Playhouse it received four stars from *The Times* and five stars from *The Daily Express,* and has been nominated for an Off West End Award for Best New Play.

She is currently the Tour Director on *The Comedy About a Bank Robbery* (Mischief Theatre/Kenny Wax Productions) and is Associate Director on the same play at the Criterion Theatre in the West End. Previous productions include *Exactly Like You*, which received four stars from *The Scotsman* at last year's Edinburgh festival. During its run at the Edinburgh Festival in 2014, it was announced as one of the first six winners of a Scotsman Fringe First Awards. Kirsty is Artistic Director of Waifs + Strays' theatre company and an Associate Director for nabokov Theatre & Theatre Uncut. She was selected for the National Theatre Studio Directors Course '15, was shortlisted for the JP Morgan Emerging Directors Award in 2013 and was selected as a 2012 finalist for the JMK Young Directors Award.

JOHN WEBBER (WRITER)

John studied drama at the University of Wales and acting at the Royal Welsh College of Music and Drama. His acting career started with Young People's Theatre, working on new plays and devised pieces which then toured. As an actor he has worked at the Royal National Theatre as well as at regional theatres around the UK and television credits include the *EastEnders*, *Coronation Street* and *Doctor Foster*. His short plays have been staged at Theatre503 and *REAP*, his first full-length play, reached the latter stages of the Bruntwood Prize, the Papatango Prize, BBC Writersroom and was selected for the Arcola Theatre's PlayWROUGHT festival. *Spiderfly* was longlisted for the Bruntwood Prize, selected for the Park Theatre's Script Accelerator Scheme and has had the support of Old Vic New Voices. John was a BRIT Program Guest Artist at the University of South Florida in early 2019.

LIZZY LEECH (SET & COSTUME DESIGNER)

Lizzy trained at Bristol Old Vic Theatre School and studied English Literature at Warwick University.

Recent designs include: *To My Younger Self* (Synergy Theatre); *A Table Tennis Play* (Walrus Theare/ Theatre Royal Plymouth); *The Merchant of Venice* (Stafford Festival Shakespeare;, *Cymbeline* (Royal Central School of Speech and Drama); *The Butterfly Lion* (The Barn Theatre, Cirencester); *Hansel and Gretel, Fairytale Detectives* (Theatr Clwyd); *Songlines* (HighTide Theatre); *The Leftovers* (Leicester Curve); *A Girl in School Uniform (walks into a bar)* (New Diorama Theatre and Leeds Playhouse); *Alby the Penguin Saves Christmas* (Oxford Playhouse); *Noye's Fludde* (Blackheath Halls Children's Opera); *Don Giovanni* (Waterperry Opera Festival); *Vanity Fair* (Middle Temple Hall); *Love for Love* and *The Heresy of Love* (Bristol Old Vic).

As Assistant Designer: *Pericles, Beginning* (National Theatre/West End); *Macbeth* (Royal Shakespeare Company); *A Tale of Two Cities* and *Oliver Twist* (Regent's Park Open Air Theatre).

DOMINIC BRENNAN (SOUND DESIGNER)

Dominic Brennan is a Offie-winning composer and sound designer with a background in electronic music. Previous shows include *Cuckoo* (Metal Rabbit/Soho Theatre); *We're Staying Right Here* (Metal Rabbit/Park Theatre); *Pandora* (Etch/The Pleasance); *The Universal Machine* (New Diorama Theatre) and *Digs* (Theatre With Legs/The Pleasance). In 2017 he won the Off-West End Award for Sound Design for his work on *Down & Out in Paris and London (*New Diorama Theatre/Greenwich Theatre*)*. He has also written music for adverts and short films and recently created a sound installation at the Princess of Wales Conservatory in Kew Gardens.

PETER SMALL (LIGHTING DESIGNER)

Peter is an Offie and Theatre & Technology Award nominated lighting designer working across theatre, dance and opera.

Recent credits include *Baby Reindeer* (Bush/Edinburgh Fringe); *Square Go* (UK tour/59E59 Theater New York/Edinburgh Fringe); *LIT* (Clapham Omnibus/HighTide Aldeburgh Festival/Nottingham Playhouse); *Angry Alan* (Soho Theatre/Aspen Fringe); *Do Our Best* (Edinburgh Fringe); *Radio* (Arcola); *Ad Libido* (Soho Theatre/VAULT Festival/Edinburgh Fringe); *YOU STUPID DARKNESS!* (Theatre Royal Plymouth); Paines Plough Roundabout Tour productions 2017–19, including the Offie Nominated *Black Mountain*; *A Girl In School Uniform (walks into a bar)* (Offie and Theatre & Technology Award Nominated – New Diorama) and *All or Nothing* (West End/tour).

Upcoming projects include productions with New Diorama and Paines Plough, among others.

METAL RABBIT PRODUCTIONS

Metal Rabbit was established in 2012 by George Warren & Martha Wilson. Its first production was Ernest Hemingway's *Fiesta* in February 2013 at the Trafalgar Studios, followed by *Johnny Got His Gun* in May 2014 at the Southwark Playhouse.

In early 2018 the company refocused its vision under the new leadership of George Warren and Sofi Berenger focussing on providing high-quality productions by first-time playwrights on current political and social topics. It has since debuted the work of Lisa Carroll (*Cuckoo*, Soho Theatre 2018) and Henry Devas (*We're Staying Right Here*, Park Theatre 2019) and *Spiderfly* will be the company's third production under the new direction.

GEORGE WARREN (PRODUCER)

George Warren worked as a script developer for Scottish Screen, Summit Entertainment (now Lionsgate) and Nutopia, and Sky Drama.

From 2015–2018 he produced for international sensation Gandini Juggling, for whom he produced touring shows *Sigma* (premier Assembly Edinburgh 2017) and *Spring* (premier Saddler's Wells 2018), and the company's first tour of the USA with their show 4x4: Ephemeral Architectures.

Further work includes with puppet company Monstro Theatre, for who he produced two tours of their show Bookstory and their new show *The Dong with a Luminous Nose* at the Little Angel Theatre in September 2019 with over 100 puppets, and sonic theatre company ERRATICA.

Since founding Metal Rabbit he has worked across all shows as script developer and executive producer.

SOFI BERENGER (PRODUCER)

Sofi Berenger is an Offie Award-winning theatre producer from Melbourne, Australia. Currently, she is the general manager at Olivier Award nominated Les Enfants Terribles and Les Petits Theatre Company. Previously, Sofi was the general manager at Iris Theatre where she now sits on the board of trustees and producer for London's Free Open Air Theatre Season at The Scoop.

In addition to producing and general managing for Metal Rabbit Productions and Les Enfants Terribles, Sofi is also the producer for Pleasance Theatre associate artists Wound Up Theatre and co-producer with Monstro Theatre on *The Dong with a Luminous Nose*.

Since joining Metal Rabbit Productions, Sofi produces and general manages all productions.

OLIVER SEYMOUR (ASSISTANT PRODUCER)

With a background in theatre and speech radio production, Oli's recent theatrical projects include *Human*, an experimental music/theatre act, and *Petrichor* (ZENDEH), a devised piece. He co-wrote the comedy *Wishing on a Stopgap*, which received four-star reviews at Edinburgh Fringe in 2018. As well as assistant producing this current run, Oli worked on *Spiderfly* in its earlier development at Park Theatre.

He's also produced on award-winning radio series, including *Something Understood* (BBC Radio 4) and *Pause for Thought* (BBC Radio 2). Other popular radio projects he's assisted on include *The Walk* (BBC Radio 4), *The Keith Urban Playlist* and *Brad Paisley: This is Country Music* (BBC Radio 2).

NOTE ON PLAY

When we were at the later stages of getting this play ready, I was asked to explain what a spiderfly was, which kind of flummoxed me.

It's a made-up word – I thought – obvs. And also, it clearly refers to the outlook of one of the characters in the play – if you'd read it – that some relationships have a predatory dynamic which may be dangerous for at least one of the people involved and this is pre-ordained. My triggered reaction to the question clearly says more about me than the question itself.

But thinking about it more afterwards, the word spiderfly started to mean more to me than just being a cool title for a play – which is all I thought it was, tbh. Maybe it describes – actually – the mood that settled over us all back in 2016 when the play's first draft was written, the year of the EU referendum and the Trump victory, then the warmest year on record. Maybe it's a word that perfectly describes two fixed and oppositional world views smashing together and being held in a toxic and tangled co-existence. And maybe it resembles how many of us feel now – that due to our own beliefs feeling so true and inherent and immovable, we've become stuck in some knotty grip with our similarly motivated opponents and now are faced with the possibility that it's in fact all of us who might end up dead in a ditch.

And if this is true, maybe collectively we need to go on a journey much like Esther in *Spiderfly* and like her understand that many of our absolute certainties are not that certain nor can they survive seismic changes to our worlds – and only by letting go of some of them, even some deeply held certainties around how we see ourselves, like Esther does, can we imagine and then create some new truths together.

John Webber,
October 2019

THEATRE 503

Theatre503 is the home of new writers and a launchpad for the artists who bring their words to life. We are pioneers in supporting new writers and a champion of their role in the theatre ecology. We find exceptional playwrights who will define the canon for the next generation. Learning and career development are at the core of what we do. We stage the work of more debut and emerging writers than any other theatre in the country. In the last year alone we staged over 60 productions featuring 133 writers from short plays to full runs of superb drama and launching over 1,000 artists in the process. We passionately believe the most important element in a writer's development is to see their work developed through to a full production on stage, performed to the highest professional standard in front of an audience.

Over the last decade many first-time writers have gone on to establish a career in the industry thanks to the support of Theatre503: Tom Morton-Smith (**Oppenheimer**, RSC & West End), Anna Jordan (Bruntwood Prize Winner for **Yen**, Royal Exchange, Royal Court and Broadway), Vinay Patel (writer of the BAFTA-winning **Murdered By My Father**), Katori Hall (**Mountaintop**, 503, West End & Broadway – winner of 503's first Olivier Award) and Jon Brittain (**Rotterdam** – winner of our second Olivier Award in 2017).

THEATRE503 TEAM

Artistic Director	Lisa Spirling
Executive Director	Andrew Shepherd
Producer	Gabrielle Leadbeater
Literary Manager	Steve Harper
General Manager	Molly Jones
Marketing Coordinator	Jennifer Oliver
Technical Manager	Alex Farrell
Literary Associate	Lauretta Barrow
Box Office Supervisor	Daisy Milner
Resident Assistant Producers	Frankie Greig and Beth Cooper

THEATRE503 BOARD

Erica Whyman OBE (Chair)
Royce Bell (Vice Chair)
Chris Campbell
Joachim Fleury
Celine Gagnon
Eleanor Lloyd
Marcus Markou
Geraldine Sharpe-Newton
Jack Tilbury
Roy Williams OBE

THEATRE503 VOLUNTEERS

Hannah Bates, Suzie Brewis, Georgia Cusworth, Debra Dempster, Rachel Gemaehling, Gareth Jones, Tom Lynam, Graham McCulloch, Tom Mellors, Annabel Pemberton, Meli Pinkerton, Hannah Randall, Gaye Russell, Hannah Sands, Caroline Summers, Thanos Topouzis, Melisa Tehrani, Camilla Walters.

SPIDERFLY

John Webber

Acknowledgements

For their help in bringing this play to the stage, I'd like to give special thanks to: George Warren, Sofi Berenger, Oli Seymour and all at Metal Rabbit; Ruth D'Silva, Eduard Lewis, Felix Scott, Lily McLeish, Tom Mothersdale and Kirsty Patrick Ward; Melli Marie and the Park Theatre Script Accelerator; Old Vic New Voices and Old Vic Workrooms; Lisa Spirling, Steve Harper and all at Theatre503.

J.W.

4

Characters

ESTHER, *early thirties*
KEITH, *late twenties*
CHRIS, *early thirties*

Chris and Keith can be played by the same actor.

This text went to press before the end of rehearsals and so may differ slightly from the play as performed.

1.

Evening.

ESTHER *stands.*

ESTHER. I'm nervous.

> *Beat.*

> I'm waiting. I'm –

> *Beat.*

> and it's –

> *Beat.*

> I want a cigarette.

> *Beat.*

> I really want a cigarette.

> *Beat.*

> I'm not going to – I don't smoke – I'm not a smoker.
> Any more.

> *Beat.*

> You're right by the way. Showing too much cleavage is – you
> know what I mean? I've gone for something – I need to look
> nice, create the right impression, show myself to be, you know
> – whatever I'm feeling inside, I need to look – well – I don't
> want to look like – I don't want to look dumb. Who wants to
> meet someone who looks dumb? Actually, lots of guys. I need
> to look intelligent but not too scary. Happy. I need to look
> happy. I need to look happy. Nicotine-free, obviously. Free –
> just – free of stuff and baggage, you know? Look free, happy
> and in the moment. Look like everything has been left behind.
> Look like – new. A new start. That's what I've got to look like.

> *Beat.*

That's who I've got to be now.

Beat.

Jesus.

Beat.

Okay.

Beat.

2.

Day.

KEITH *and* ESTHER *sit*.

Silence.

KEITH. It is good to meet you at last.

ESTHER. Yes.

KEITH. I'm Keith.

ESTHER. I know.

    Beat.

    It's awkward.

KEITH. You like a drink?

ESTHER. I'm okay for now.

KEITH. I can get one.

ESTHER. I'm fine.

KEITH. Some water.

ESTHER. No.

    He gestures to someone, holding two fingers up.

KEITH. Usually they're like eagle-eyes, staring through your head, but now –

Beat.

You look –

ESTHER. What?

KEITH. Are you going to take this the wrong way?

ESTHER. That depends on –

KEITH. You look nice.

ESTHER. Right.

Beat.

KEITH. You look nice.

Beat.

Do you like spiders?

ESTHER. No.

KEITH. Oh.

Beat.

ESTHER. Why?

KEITH. I have this spider back at mine.

ESTHER. At yours?

KEITH. He's a big bleeder.

ESTHER. Right.

KEITH. I live with him –

ESTHER. I said, I don't really –

KEITH. Yes, I know what you mean, but, look – no – you don't want to know –

ESTHER. No.

Beat.

KEITH. I gave it a job. I said to myself, he's eating the flies, he's earned the right to be here, doing me a service, welcome.

Beat.

ESTHER. Sorry –

KEITH. No – you're right –

ESTHER. it's one of the things I don't like about autumn –

KEITH. Yeah?

ESTHER. The trees look lovely and so on, but –

KEITH. Yeah –

ESTHER. I don't like it when the spiders all come indoors –

KEITH. Yeah.

ESTHER. I really don't like it when they leave their web to go and build another one, you know how they do that?

KEITH. Yes.

ESTHER. The old one gets full of dust and horrible. My mum used to laugh at me because as a kid I hated dust –

KEITH. Dust?

ESTHER. It's true. I always liked to tidy things up. Mum joked about it all the time, when I was little. She'd probably say now that's why I turned out as I did and ended up doing the job I do.

KEITH. What do you do?

ESTHER. Couples' counsellor.

Beat.

KEITH. I don't know what that is.

Beat.

Sounds like you get on with her then.

ESTHER. Who?

KEITH. Your mum.

ESTHER. Don't you?

KEITH. She was just there, wasn't she? Mums are just there when you're a kid, aren't they? You don't even notice them.

ESTHER. My mum wasn't.

KEITH. No?

ESTHER. I was twelve when –

Beat.

KEITH. Sorry about that.

Beat.

My mum hasn't spoken to me for a year. Not a word. And my dad – I was twelve when he disappeared – that's weird, isn't it? Both of us, both of us twelve.

Beat.

He got with a girl half his age. I used to see them walking around holding hands. Like, I mean, come on. I once saw them kissing, like full-on tongues, in a bus shelter. Yeah. Terrible, right?

Beat.

Houseflies are disgusting though.

ESTHER. Pardon?

KEITH. Going back to spiders.

ESTHER. I don't –

KEITH. Yeah – I know – I'm just saying – you can find it pretty educational, you know, seeing the fly land in the web, he runs out, and grabs it. He poisons it, or whatever he does, you know, stabs it, I think they stab things. Then he wraps it up all tight.

Beat.

No – there I go again –

Beat.

What I'm saying is that houseflies are horrible – it might help change your view of spiders –

ESTHER. Yes –

KEITH. you know?

ESTHER. How do you know the spider is a he?

Awkwardness.

Couples come to me and talk about what's going on for them. I kind of – I – well – mediate, in a way. I'm cheaper than a lawyer, I guess. It's not rocket science – things get messy – confused – during marital split-ups. You can lose sight of things. Sometimes they want to understand who the other person is now, who they are themselves even – or find a way to carry on – but some people just want to move on and forget all about the past.

Beat.

KEITH. Like therapy.

ESTHER. I'm not a therapist.

KEITH. A bit like it though.

ESTHER. You have to study much more to be a therapist.

KEITH. I've got a therapist.

ESTHER. Yes?

KEITH. I'm a bit reluctant to be honest.

ESTHER. Oh, therapy is useful.

KEITH. Nah.

ESTHER. I did it last year, it was really helpful to have someone on your side, you know? I've done it before – in my line of work – you know – it's useful to have done it but –

Beat.

You don't need to hear this.

KEITH. They never want to talk about what you want, though. I wanted my woman to discuss evil, like does evil exist? Are people born with it? You know? I bet women don't ask their therapist about that much. She said she didn't think it would be a good use of our time.

Pause.

I don't know what happened to that water.

ESTHER. It doesn't matter.

KEITH. My throat's dry.

ESTHER. I'm fine.

Silence.

KEITH. Shall we start again?

ESTHER. Start again?

KEITH. Yes.

ESTHER. From where?

KEITH. Just from when you sat down.

ESTHER. I don't want to go back.

KEITH. I try to stay in shape. Do you? You look like you do. I'm trying to look like I used to – but – things change, don't they?

Beat.

Where are you from?

Beat.

We've started again.

ESTHER. I can't –

KEITH. I –

Beat.

ESTHER. What?

Beat.

KEITH. I don't know what you want from me –

Pause.

ESTHER. Okay, let's start again.

KEITH. The mood has changed.

ESTHER. Ask me your question again.

KEITH. What question?

ESTHER. I'm from Romford.

KEITH. Okay.

ESTHER. Yes.

KEITH. That's what I read.

ESTHER. That's where we all lived.

KEITH. I remember now.

Beat.

I used to go to Romford a lot.

Beat.

I was just thinking about dating sites and they even have these sites in the States, you know, online dating sites – for prisoners –

ESTHER. Do they?

KEITH. and these sites have the usual, like, profile things with pictures and stuff and you click on them and they tell you a bit about the person and you can then choose who you want to contact.

ESTHER. How do you know about it?

KEITH. It's a bit weird, though, isn't it?

ESTHER. Have you seen one?

KEITH. I have to be honest – just for research purposes.

ESTHER. Research?

KEITH. Seeing what's out there.

ESTHER. And?

KEITH. Well, you – see a picture you like – they look cute or whatever –

ESTHER. Yes –

KEITH. and they say things like 'looking for sweet love' –

ESTHER. nothing wrong with that –

KEITH. but then you read their release date and it's, like, in twenty years –

ESTHER. that's sad –

KEITH. but they don't tell you what they're in for, which is a real no-no for me, because you don't get twenty years for shoplifting.

ESTHER. I've always thought that's what happens on all dating sites anyway. You see someone's picture but it's actually for some unknown reason you're pulled to them –

KEITH. Yeah.

ESTHER. it's only when you meet up with them in the flesh that you find out what's really going on.

KEITH. You'll get this then – my therapist has got this theory about how people decide who they want to get it on with, like who is their soulmate, yeah? Not consciously, but, like, subconsciously. She says we have these, like these filters to sift out the wheat – first off, there's – oh I can't remember what she was going on about but at the bottom of it we basically sift through all the girls we fancy until we find the one who is as messed up as us – we have this like antennae, like this sense before someone has even said a word – we're drawn to it – drawn to that bit of our own mess that lives in the other person – I mean, we all do it – she holds to this – it stuck with me.

ESTHER. That seems unbelievably sad to me.

KEITH. Yeah.

ESTHER. Doesn't it?

KEITH. I didn't say I believed it.

ESTHER. Maybe it's true.

KEITH. Do you think?

ESTHER. Doesn't say much for love, though.

KEITH. It says love sucks.

ESTHER. I mean – I believe in psychology and – but – there has to be room for something else – doesn't there? I'd like to believe that we are attracted to what's good in someone – yes? That we have –

KEITH. an antennae –

ESTHER. an antennae – yes – for good stuff as much as – the rest. I'd rather believe in that.

KEITH. I couldn't agree with you more.

ESTHER. Really?

KEITH. My therapist can be a downer like that sometimes.

ESTHER. She's just doing her job.

KEITH. Yes.

Pause.

ESTHER. I want to say something.

Beat.

As soon as I first saw you I knew you were the one. I don't know how. There was a feeling. And actually – I don't know if I've felt that way before about anyone – honestly – I fell for my ex-husband pretty quickly but even that didn't have – this speed – this sickening feeling – this rush – the room disappeared and there was just you.

Beat.

I knew it was you.

Beat.

I hate you – I hated you – I had a year of being in pieces and all that kept me together was my hatred of you. But – you're not going to make me feel that way any more. I never thought it was in me to do this but – it's what I was taught – so I will do it – I've worked on it and I will do it – I don't want to be someone bitter – full of hate – no – that's not who I'm going to be – I want –

Beat.

oh, Jesus, this is hard – so – I forgive you.

Beat.

I forgive you.

Silence.

KEITH. Full marks to you. People don't really do that any more. Out of fashion, isn't it? Forgiveness. Sorry if this is out of turn but – it's like giving up. It's like giving up on something. I don't think I could do it, actually. Because I never give up. It's true. I don't give up. It's not in my nature.

3.

Evening.

ESTHER *stands with a fixed smile on her face.*

She smiles fixedly for one minute.

Her smile fades.

She forces herself to smile again.

4.

Day.

ESTHER *sits and* CHRIS *stands*.

ESTHER. Yes?

CHRIS. Hi.

ESTHER. Hi.

CHRIS. You're –

ESTHER. Yes.

CHRIS. Esther?

ESTHER. Yes.

CHRIS. Great.

ESTHER. I'm Esther.

CHRIS. You look exactly like your profile.

ESTHER. That's good.

CHRIS. Yes.

ESTHER. Good.

   Beat.

CHRIS. God – sorry – I'm –

ESTHER. Late –

CHRIS. Am I?

ESTHER. I think so –

CHRIS. What time is it?

ESTHER. what time did we say?

CHRIS. God – sorry –

ESTHER. Don't worry –

CHRIS. No – sorry –

ESTHER. you're here now –

CHRIS. I hate being the late one.

ESTHER. really.

CHRIS. I meant to set off at half-past –

ESTHER. Really?

CHRIS. but then it was twenty-to and –

ESTHER. You meant to set off at half-past?

CHRIS. Yes –

ESTHER. Oh, well –

CHRIS. What?

ESTHER. in that case –

CHRIS. What?

ESTHER. if you meant to set off at half-past –

CHRIS. You mean it's not okay?

ESTHER. you're obviously not treating this date with due seriousness.

Beat.

I'm pulling your leg.

CHRIS. Oh.

ESTHER. I was trying to break the ice.

CHRIS. Okay.

ESTHER. I'm often the late one too.

CHRIS. Oh – ha – good.

Beat.

ESTHER. Oh, no, did you just see me pulling faces just now?

CHRIS. No.

ESTHER. You can say if you did.

CHRIS. I've just got here.

ESTHER. That would have been embarrassing.

CHRIS. What were you doing?

ESTHER. It was this smiling thing.

CHRIS. What smiling thing?

ESTHER. Oh, God –

CHRIS. What?

ESTHER. I do it before any stressful situation, makes me feel better.

Beat.

CHRIS. Why do you need to feel better?

ESTHER. Oh – wow.

CHRIS. What?

ESTHER. Do we want to go there –

CHRIS. Where?

ESTHER. on a first date?

CHRIS. It's all about getting to know each other, right?

Beat.

Shall we start again?

ESTHER. Okay.

CHRIS. So my name is Chris.

ESTHER. I know.

CHRIS. Sorry – of course –

ESTHER. You apologise a lot.

CHRIS. Do I?

ESTHER. It's endearing.

CHRIS. That's terrible.

ESTHER. Is it?

CHRIS. Who wants to be endearing on a first date?

ESTHER. No one.

CHRIS. Exactly.

ESTHER. You want to be –

CHRIS. Charismatic.

ESTHER. What?

CHRIS. Charismatic.

Beat.

Yeah – so – anyway –

ESTHER. You were starting again.

CHRIS. Yes – so – I've got this new way of introducing yourself – can I show you?

ESTHER. Sure.

CHRIS. It's – so – you don't do the factual stuff, you know, place of birth, age or –

ESTHER. Star sign.

CHRIS. Sure, all that stuff. I don't think it helps.

ESTHER. Not that I believe in star signs.

CHRIS. You introduce yourself but without mentioning any facts – like – I believe in art – it's my religion – no facts – you see? Some people go to church – but – I go to art galleries or anywhere that has good art, clearly there's a difference between good art and bad art – I stand in front of this art and usually it dawns on me that all these artists have completely different ideas about the world and then – I have this – overwhelming feeling – that there is nothing – it's all just comforting meaningless patterns we dream up to make ourselves feel better – I end up in these big white rooms feeling lost – nothing is fixed, we're floating in space, but – Jesus, it's okay – it's okay that nothing means anything, just look at how beautiful these patterns on the wall are – I feel different then, you know?

Beat.

ESTHER. Are you depressed?

CHRIS. Sorry, is that depressing?

ESTHER. Shall we change the subject?

CHRIS. Really?

ESTHER. Everyone spends so much time working everything out from scratch but everything is set already, don't you think? Taking on board the lessons from ancient history is already difficult enough, like how do you actually keep yourself being a good person, you know, according to the rules of the Bible, say, when you are surrounded by everything that goes on in the world? The answer has been out there for centuries. Coming up with an empty new shape, that's just trying to be a clever know-it-all, thinking you're cleverer than the wisest people in history, like –

CHRIS. Okay.

ESTHER. like believing you're cleverer than Jesus or something.

Beat.

CHRIS. Do you think I'm a know-it-all?

ESTHER. No –

CHRIS. I've upset you.

ESTHER. no – God – I don't know why I mentioned Jesus.

CHRIS. It's okay –

ESTHER. I grew up with these things.

CHRIS. it's not a problem –

ESTHER. I'm nervous.

Beat.

I bet you don't get this response when you try that gallery speech with other dates.

CHRIS. Gallery speech?

ESTHER. No – I – sorry –

CHRIS. Was that what it sounded like?

ESTHER. It did sound – a bit –

CHRIS. Oh, shit – sorry – I guess I'm a bit nervous too.

Beat.

ESTHER. Facts are important, though, aren't they?

CHRIS. Sure.

ESTHER. They do tell you – something.

CHRIS. I'm not saying they don't.

ESTHER. Like, for instance, say you were divorced –

CHRIS. Divorced?

ESTHER. Just say that was factually true –

CHRIS. Okay.

ESTHER. it would say something about who you are.

CHRIS. Okay, well, maybe –

ESTHER. No?

CHRIS. maybe –

ESTHER. Don't you think?

CHRIS. I mean, doesn't it just say that once I was married and now I'm not?

Beat.

ESTHER. I am divorced.

CHRIS. Sorry?

ESTHER. Is that a problem?

CHRIS. No –

ESTHER. Really?

CHRIS. Jesus, no –

ESTHER. You don't seem sure.

CHRIS. Was it on your profile?

ESTHER. No.

CHRIS. Do you have kids?

ESTHER. No.

CHRIS. That's a relief.

ESTHER. What?

CHRIS. No –

ESTHER. Don't you like kids?

CHRIS. No, no – I mean – yes.

ESTHER. Okay.

CHRIS. Sorry – look – I'm divorced too.

ESTHER. Oh.

CHRIS. Yes.

ESTHER. Was that on your profile?

CHRIS. Sorry.

ESTHER. Jesus, what does that say about us?

CHRIS. It says we're liars –

ESTHER. Don't say that.

CHRIS. Sorry.

Beat.

Was it amicable?

ESTHER. Is it ever amicable?

CHRIS. Well, my ex and I – well – it was kind of amicable.

ESTHER. Really?

CHRIS. We felt like we'd moved apart.

ESTHER. That's sad.

CHRIS. Like we are different people now.

ESTHER. It's not on my profile because of what it says about me.

CHRIS. What do you think it says?

ESTHER. Hopefully it says my husband was an insensitive arse.

CHRIS. Or it says we're failures in love.

ESTHER. That's really not how I want to be seen.

CHRIS. Well, it wasn't an ambition of mine, either, like –

ESTHER. Jesus –

CHRIS. like I sat in school –

ESTHER. no –

CHRIS. like I sat in school and thought I'd love to be a thirty-something divorced guy with my stuff in a suitcase and renting a mate's room in Canada Water.

ESTHER. Is that what you are?

CHRIS. Yeah.

ESTHER. God –

CHRIS. Thanks.

ESTHER. No, no, I mean both of us. It's hard to put it all behind you.

CHRIS. What was hard – the divorce was hard – it really changes your idea of yourself for a while.

ESTHER. Oh, I totally get that. It's been a hard year for me. You'd think being brought up with Jesus it would help, like he's sat deep inside you waiting to support you or something but he wasn't – it's weird how the things you try desperately to hold on to are the first to go.

Beat.

I must be the worst date ever.

CHRIS. No – no –

ESTHER. The worst thing you can mention on a first date is
    Jesus, right?

CHRIS. I'm not going anywhere.

Beat.

ESTHER. Look, do you fancy finding somewhere to eat?

CHRIS. There is this great Thai place near here.

ESTHER. That would be great.

Beat.

5.

Evening.

ESTHER *is smiling fixedly and looking straight ahead.*

She stops smiling.

ESTHER. It's not working – the smiling thing – you know, the
    smiling thing? – I'm on my own, yes, I'm still waiting –
    I watched it on the internet. If you make yourself smile for
    two minutes, just the physical act of smiling, whether you
    want to smile or not – it chemically changes your brain, it's
    scientifically proven apparently. Does any of this ring a bell?
    It releases this happy drug into your bloodstream. It can
    change your brain and make you feel okay. You can change
    your biological make-up by adopting this one facial
    expression. She has a PhD this woman. I don't feel any
    happier. Maybe I should try it for longer than two minutes.

She smiles fixedly.

6.

Day.

ESTHER *and* KEITH *sit*.

KEITH. Drink?

ESTHER. I'm okay.

KEITH. I can get one.

ESTHER. It's fine.

KEITH. Some water.

ESTHER. No.

   Beat.

KEITH. No.

   Beat.

   You look nice.

   Beat.

ESTHER. Thanks.

KEITH. I never know – you know –

ESTHER. No.

KEITH. Compliments.

ESTHER. Compliments?

KEITH. Women like them.

ESTHER. Do they?

KEITH. Oh, yeah.

ESTHER. Right.

KEITH. It's something I practise, you know –

ESTHER. Practise?

KEITH. Yeah –

ESTHER. It makes it sound like it's not genuine.

KEITH. No, no – I'm saying I've never been good at it and women like it, so I'm making a special effort to say it if I think it. Like practising a new skill.

ESTHER. Right.

KEITH. You look nice.

Beat.

How was the drive?

ESTHER. It was fine.

Beat.

KEITH. I love driving. Don't you?

ESTHER. Not really.

KEITH. No?

ESTHER. It just gets you from A to B.

KEITH. Oh, no, that's a shame.

ESTHER. My dad was into Formula 1, which I hate.

KEITH. I'm an only child, me.

ESTHER. Yes?

KEITH. Spoilt little fucker, I reckon.

Beat.

What's it like having a big family?

ESTHER. I don't have a big family.

KEITH. Two of you, right?

Beat.

ESTHER. Yes.

KEITH. That's big to me. And then with your mum and dad, that's four, right? I'm a singleton. That's the word my woman used.

ESTHER. Who's your woman?

KEITH. My therapist.

ESTHER. Oh, yes.

KEITH. I told you about her.

ESTHER. You did.

KEITH. I tell you the trouble with therapists – they expect you to do all the talking.

Beat.

I did driving for a living.

ESTHER. Black cabs.

KEITH. I loved the nights. The quiet. The freedom. Driving around in the dark, the street lamps. Cruising through the red lights sometimes. Sometimes going up the West End to pick up some party girls all laughing and that. Bringing them back to Barking, poor cows.

Beat.

You came back.

ESTHER. I nearly didn't.

KEITH. I thought you would –

ESTHER. Maybe I should go.

KEITH. Go where?

ESTHER. Go home.

KEITH. You've just got here –

ESTHER. I know but –

KEITH. and you don't like driving.

Beat.

My dad was a driver. HGV. He got done for short delivering. Know what that is? Basically, like, if you've got a pallet of ten boxes, you take them to the shops and instead of delivering the ten, you deliver nine, and after doing say ten short deliveries you've got like a pallet of ten all for yourself.

ESTHER. And then what?

KEITH. You sell them.

ESTHER. Didn't people notice?

KEITH. The thing is you'll never guess what was in the boxes. Ice-cream cones. I mean, that's a slow way to your first million.

ESTHER. That's funny.

KEITH. Once it all went digital, he got fucked. Got sent down for a year. My mum told me he was on holiday. She cried for weeks when he was convicted. I didn't even bat an eye.

Beat.

What about your dad?

ESTHER. I don't –

KEITH. Do you remember much?

ESTHER. He's still alive.

KEITH. Yeah?

Beat.

ESTHER. One thing, after my mum – I did the cooking but on Sundays my dad insisted on cooking breakfast. It was always tinned tomatoes on white toast. Loads of butter and it got all soggy but I loved it. If we were good he gave us crispy bacon on top too.

Beat.

KEITH. Sounds alright that.

ESTHER. The food was.

KEITH. What happened to your mum?

ESTHER. I don't want to talk about my mum.

Beat.

KEITH. Did you want some water?

KEITH *signals for water.*

They're so slack here.

Pause.

We don't have to talk about anything.

ESTHER. That doesn't make sense.

KEITH. Why not?

ESTHER. I took the day off work.

KEITH. We can sit here quiet.

Beat.

We can talk about my family then.

ESTHER. If that's what you want.

KEITH. Maybe that's why you're here –

ESTHER. I don't know why I'm here –

KEITH. You want to find out about me.

ESTHER. No.

KEITH. Spend some time then.

ESTHER. No.

KEITH. Well, I did wonder –

ESTHER. Wonder what?

KEITH. After what you said last time.

Beat.

Are you religious?

ESTHER. I went to a convent school.

KEITH. That's why all the forgiveness stuff then.

ESTHER. It's ingrained.

KEITH. Yeah?

Beat.

ESTHER. Mrs Moore taught us to sing 'Onward Christian
Soldiers'. It's not very Catholic. She was weird like that.
This is primary school. She taught us to sing the line 'With
the cross of Jesus going on before' by slapping the backs of
our heads on the 'Je' of Jesus and our bum on the 'sus'.
Je-sus. Like that.

KEITH. Sounds pervy.

ESTHER. It was to make sure we got the key change.

KEITH. Still sounds pervy.

ESTHER. It was the beginning of the end for me. Like
something I thought was part of me suddenly seemed stupid
– like how can you use Jesus to hurt kids, you know?

KEITH. Yeah.

ESTHER. So he isn't this thing inside me any more – Jesus – he
is a thing that other people use – to do what they want.

KEITH. Yeah?

ESTHER. Like my dad. It's him that sent me there.

Beat.

KEITH. I hated school too. That's another thing we have in
common.

Beat.

ESTHER. I don't know why I came back.

Pause.

KEITH. My mum lives in Dagenham.

ESTHER. Yes.

KEITH. It's a total shithole.

ESTHER. Is it?

KEITH. Total.

ESTHER. So you moved?

KEITH. Yeah, to Barking.

Beat.

If you knew Barking you'd find that funny.

ESTHER. Did you go back to visit?

KEITH. I haven't seen her for over a year.

ESTHER. Does that bother you?

KEITH. Would it bother you?

ESTHER. If I was in your position –

KEITH. If you were in my position?

ESTHER. I'd want a visit –

KEITH. Well, she hasn't.

ESTHER. I'd want my mum to visit me.

KEITH. She doesn't want to –

ESTHER. Because she's upset?

KEITH. She'd be more than upset.

ESTHER. How do you know?

KEITH. I know her.

ESTHER. What is she then?

KEITH. I don't know.

ESTHER. What do you think?

KEITH. Who knows?

ESTHER. Not upset, so what?

KEITH. Fucked up.

Beat.

I'm not good with words.

ESTHER. Is that what you think?

KEITH. What is this?

ESTHER. I'm just asking.

KEITH. It feels like an interrogation.

ESTHER. It's not.

Beat.

KEITH. I could murder a fag.

Beat.

Have you got one?

ESTHER. I don't smoke.

KEITH. I've run out.

ESTHER. I can't help.

Beat.

I gave up.

KEITH. I love it.

ESTHER. I loved it too.

KEITH. Cup of coffee –

ESTHER. in the morning.

KEITH. Why'd you stop then?

ESTHER. I don't know. Health.

KEITH. You've got to have some pleasures in life.

ESTHER. I could murder a fag too.

Pause.

KEITH. My spider shed his skin. Actually, spiders don't shed skins. They moult. Yeah. And it's not skin. It's a – it's a – when they moult they pump up their muscles like bodybuilders – seriously – to force it off, the old one. They're knackered afterwards, so they find somewhere to hide to avoid predators who might eat them when they're resting. I found my spider's old skin in the corner.

Beat.

ESTHER. Exoskeleton.

KEITH. Exoskeleton.

Beat.

I thought he'd gone but no. There he was, bigger than ever.

Beat.

Can you bring some fags when you come next time?

Beat.

If you want to come again, that is.

Beat.

If you want to feel useful.

7.

Day.

CHRIS *and* ESTHER *stand but apart.*

ESTHER. I can't see you.

CHRIS. Damn.

ESTHER. Are you there?

 Beat.

CHRIS. Hi.

ESTHER. I lost you.

CHRIS. It's the wifi.

ESTHER. Where are you?

CHRIS. Still at the conference centre.

ESTHER. Oh, no.

CHRIS. Yeah, some delay with the main speaker.

ESTHER. What did you say?

CHRIS. Maybe we should just do audio.

 Beat.

ESTHER. I can see you fine now.

CHRIS. Hi.

ESTHER. Hi. What's your speech about?

CHRIS. 'Maintaining identity in a shifting reality.'

ESTHER. Oh.

CHRIS. What?

ESTHER. Sounds good.

CHRIS. I made it as punchy as I could.

ESTHER. You've frozen.

CHRIS. Have I lost you?

Beat.

ESTHER. Hello.

CHRIS. How are you?

ESTHER. I'm good, actually.

CHRIS. Listen –

ESTHER. It's okay –

CHRIS. It's been so busy –

ESTHER. You shouldn't apologise.

CHRIS. I'm sorry.

ESTHER. It's just that – on a first date –

CHRIS. Absolutely.

ESTHER. I don't normally –

CHRIS. You don't need to say –

ESTHER. I'm not someone who –

CHRIS. I know.

ESTHER. I'm not usually someone who sleeps with anyone on a first date.

CHRIS. No.

Beat.

ESTHER. Chris?

CHRIS. Yes?

ESTHER. I thought you'd frozen.

CHRIS. I'm still here.

ESTHER. It would be good to get things straight.

CHRIS. I'm in public here.

ESTHER. What?

CHRIS. It's the lobby of the conference centre.

ESTHER. I'm using public wifi too.

CHRIS. It might undermine my carefully cultivated image of the earnest academic.

Beat.

That was a joke.

ESTHER. Do you think we have anything here, Chris?

CHRIS. Do I think we have anything?

ESTHER. Yes.

CHRIS. We have something, yes.

Beat.

Actually, I think we have more than something.

ESTHER. Really?

CHRIS. You – make me feel kind of different.

ESTHER. It's just –

CHRIS. Oh God, I always do this.

ESTHER. you left me not knowing.

CHRIS. I'm trying to change –

ESTHER. Change what?

CHRIS. say what's going on for me inside –

ESTHER. Okay –

CHRIS. it's the goal I set myself.

ESTHER. Sure – I'm trying to change things up too.

CHRIS. It was amazing. Really. I'm glad I took the risk.

ESTHER. What risk?

CHRIS. That sounds terrible.

ESTHER. No – yes, actually, it kind of does.

CHRIS. I mean – you swipe left so often you wonder what it is you're looking for –

ESTHER. I guess.

CHRIS. and so with you I swiped right because you seemed different.

ESTHER. Different how?

CHRIS. I usually go for professionals, you know.

ESTHER. I'm professional.

CHRIS. Yes – no – I mean like doctors, lawyers –

ESTHER. Chris, I think you're trying to pay me a compliment but –

CHRIS. Shit –

ESTHER. it's coming out all wrong.

CHRIS. Look – sorry – what I'm trying to say is that you're really – great – it's so great how you're different from who I usually date – and I really loved our date – and what happened – and – everything – and it all feels new and different – we're both trying different things – and it's actually really pretty – cool.

Beat.

Honestly. Look –

ESTHER. It felt different for me too but I just want to avoid the mistakes – the past – you know? I'm looking to treat myself differently now, yes?

CHRIS. Yes.

Beat.

Look –

ESTHER. You need to go.

CHRIS. it's pretty public here –

ESTHER. Okay.

CHRIS. but, you know –

ESTHER. Yes?

CHRIS. I meant all of that.

ESTHER. It was nice to hear.

CHRIS. And I promise to be better at keeping in touch.

Beat.

So where are you then?

ESTHER. I'm at the motorway services.

CHRIS. Where are you going?

ESTHER. I've just been.

CHRIS. Been where?

ESTHER. I just saw that guy.

CHRIS. Which guy?

ESTHER. My sister.

CHRIS. Rachel?

ESTHER. Rachel, yes.

CHRIS. What about her?

ESTHER. Her guy.

CHRIS. He's that guy?

Beat.

ESTHER. What?

CHRIS. Nothing.

ESTHER. What's wrong?

CHRIS. I should get going.

ESTHER. I felt that I had to see him again.

CHRIS. You've seen him before?

ESTHER. Yes.

CHRIS. Did you tell me that already?

ESTHER. If you don't like this just say.

CHRIS. Sure.

Beat.

ESTHER. Shall we speak later?

CHRIS. I might have to go to dinner with some people but –

ESTHER. Chris?

CHRIS. Yeah?

Beat.

ESTHER. You know, I've been on enough of these online dates now to know there are certain things you shouldn't bring up –

CHRIS. like Jesus –

ESTHER. or my sister –

CHRIS. no, no – it's fine –

ESTHER. but there are some things unresolved with her –

CHRIS. I'm ahead of you here – we're trying out new things – it's a little weird and – maybe a bit scary – but I have to say I'm not like other guys, you know – I'm not someone who tells other people what to do –

ESTHER. Good.

CHRIS. I know guys who would put their foot down.

ESTHER. Well, women can do that too.

CHRIS. Sure, sure, but that's not me.

ESTHER. Chris – if you're unhappy –

CHRIS. I will say if it bothers me.

ESTHER. Good – thank you.

CHRIS. It's what I'm working on.

   Beat.

ESTHER. I'm really glad we managed to connect a bit today.

   Beat.

   Chris?

CHRIS. Absolutely.

8.

Evening.

ESTHER *stands.*

She takes out a packet of Marlboro cigarettes and a lighter.

She takes a cigarette from the packet and puts it in her mouth.

She strikes the lighter and holds it an inch from the end of the cigarette.

Beat.

She lights the cigarette and inhales.

9.

Day.

ESTHER *and* KEITH *sit.*

KEITH. Don't worry about it.

ESTHER. It says a lot.

KEITH. It's okay.

ESTHER. I left them on the kitchen table.

KEITH. Next time.

ESTHER. I meant to write it on my hand.

KEITH. Well, that's what I do.

ESTHER. Put a reminder on my phone.

KEITH. I'm a forgetful person as well.

ESTHER. Three packs.

KEITH. I'd forget my own head.

ESTHER. I can bring them next time.

    Beat.

KEITH. Did you get full-strength?

ESTHER. Marlboro, right?

KEITH. Red.

ESTHER. Yes.

    Beat.

KEITH. Can you bring some Rizla?

ESTHER. Rizla.

KEITH. Helps me stretch the fags out.

ESTHER. Sure.

    Beat.

KEITH. How have you been?

ESTHER. Tired.

KEITH. But you're here now.

Beat.

Just bring the fucking fags next time.

Beat.

That was a joke.

ESTHER. I will.

KEITH. No, but seriously, don't forget the Rizla.

ESTHER. I won't.

Beat.

KEITH. My mum put in a request.

ESTHER. Your mum?

KEITH. Request for a visit.

ESTHER. Really?

KEITH. What do you make of that?

ESTHER. Don't you want her to come?

KEITH. It's weird.

ESTHER. She just wants to reconnect.

KEITH. She put in for this week.

ESTHER. So you've said yes already.

KEITH. Of course I said yes, it's my mum, isn't it?

Beat.

On the wall in the front room she has this big picture of me. Me as a kid on a beach. Weston-super-Mare. Jesus, that's no place for a holiday. In the photo, I'm in a hole I've dug, up to my knees, big cheesy grin on my face, and I'm holding up my spade like a trophy or something. My coat is red. Every time I go around my mum looks at that and says I was such a sweet boy.

ESTHER. Were you?

KEITH. I don't know.

Beat.

When my mum got married to Terry, my stepdad, she set him to work on home improvements. Notice how women do that to a man.

ESTHER. Maybe men like it.

KEITH. Nah, they're keeping the peace. Terry, God bless him, repaired and creosoted this little shitty fence that went around the front yard. He looked pleased as punch afterwards, my mum too. So, when they went out, I went down the hardware and bought some paint and went back and wrote on the fence, 'Keith is best' in white paint, all over his freshly done creosote.

Beat.

How I thought I wouldn't get caught I don't know.

ESTHER. Maybe you wanted to get caught.

KEITH. Things went downhill with my mum after that.

ESTHER. This was when you were twelve?

KEITH. You sound like my therapist.

Beat.

So, tell me about yourself then.

ESTHER. Why do you want to know?

KEITH. Get to understand each other.

Beat.

Come on.

Beat.

ESTHER. My mum disappeared.

KEITH. I thought she died.

ESTHER. No.

KEITH. What do you mean she disappeared?

ESTHER. One day she was there, then the next –

KEITH. That's shit –

ESTHER. a couple of years later I found some letters – two –
I found them in the loft when I was looking for where the
Christmas presents were hidden – you know how you do that
as a kid –

KEITH. yeah –

ESTHER. in the first letter she apologised – and in the second
she said that if she didn't hear back she'd never contact me
again – it was the first time I'd seen them –

Beat.

I would never have replied anyway.

KEITH. Why not?

ESTHER. I didn't want to forgive her then.

Beat.

I haven't told anyone that.

Beat.

So, it's good that your mum is coming.

Beat.

KEITH. My mum chucked my dad out when he got back from
prison. I say chucked out, she changed the locks so when he
got back all kinds of stuff kicked off. Banging on the door,
shouting out of windows, a right scene. Neighbours. It was
funny though. I say that now but at the time I was probably
crying in a corner somewhere. That was the day I decided
to be a man. Tuck everything away. Be the master of your
own destiny.

Beat.

You had your dad still.

ESTHER. I had my dad? Not really.

KEITH. No?

ESTHER. I left.

KEITH. Yeah?

ESTHER. A few years later. Sixteen, I was. Took Rachel. Refused to look back.

KEITH. Why did you leave?

ESTHER. I don't want to talk about this.

Beat.

KEITH. With my dad gone I was like head of the house. Very nice. My mum got married a month later. Like what's that about? I hadn't even met Terry before, so it was like bye-bye. Total disconnect. I was a right terror after that.

ESTHER. I went to see your mum.

Pause.

KEITH. Why?

ESTHER. I just did.

Beat.

KEITH. You went to her house?

ESTHER. I sat in her lounge.

KEITH. In Dagenham?

ESTHER. It was homely.

Beat.

KEITH. What happened?

ESTHER. Nothing.

KEITH. Did you tell her to come and see me?

ESTHER. No.

Beat.

KEITH. You saw my picture?

ESTHER. It was on the wall.

KEITH. And then what?

ESTHER. You know for a while we just sat in silence. All I could
    hear was a clock ticking. It felt awkward but after a while
    I started to let go because she seemed so gentle and nice. It felt
    okay. It felt nice. I felt for her. She has a very warm quality.
    She spoke. What a really brave woman I was coming to see
    her. I could have been like everybody else walking on the
    other side of the street. I had more reason than anyone else to
    do that but I didn't. She nearly took the photo down. It didn't
    show who you really were she said. She's had months of
    staring at the floor when walking to the shops.

    Pause.

KEITH. Your sister –

ESTHER. What about her?

    Beat.

KEITH. I pleaded innocent.

ESTHER. I know.

KEITH. I've got nothing more to add.

ESTHER. I'm not asking you to add anything.

KEITH. No?

ESTHER. No.

KEITH. Then why are you visiting my mum?

    Pause.

ESTHER. I have this thing I do.

KEITH. What thing?

ESTHER. This woman says we can make ourselves happy just
    by changing our physicality.

KEITH. Like how?

ESTHER. By smiling.

KEITH. It doesn't take a genius to know that smiling means you're happy.

ESTHER. That's not what she's saying. You make the shape of a smile with your mouth and it tricks the brain to release hormones and you feel happier, whatever is really going on for you.

KEITH. Bollocks.

ESTHER. I like the idea.

KEITH. Total bollocks.

ESTHER. Is it?

KEITH. Fucking hormones?

ESTHER. Hormones get released by all kinds of things.

KEITH. Let's try it then.

ESTHER. No.

Beat.

KEITH. So why did you mention it?

ESTHER. I told your mum she should do it.

KEITH. Why?

ESTHER. I thought it might help.

Pause.

KEITH. Right.

Beat.

ESTHER. How's the spider?

Beat.

KEITH. Yeah, he's alright.

Beat.

I started to feed him.

Silence.

10.

Day.

CHRIS *and* ESTHER *stand apart.*

CHRIS. Where?

ESTHER. McDonald's – in Dagenham.

CHRIS. McDonald's in Dagenham?

ESTHER. I stopped off.

CHRIS. Where have you been that means stopping off in a McDonald's in Dagenham?

ESTHER. I know.

CHRIS. You get about.

ESTHER. I appreciate you calling.

CHRIS. I couldn't get hold of you earlier.

ESTHER. Shame we can't Skype.

CHRIS. It's difficult at this end.

ESTHER. You're at the airport?

CHRIS. You shouldn't eat at McDonald's.

ESTHER. I just came in for a coffee.

CHRIS. The production of beef worldwide is a serious contributor to climate change.

ESTHER. I only had a latte.

CHRIS. Sorry.

Beat.

Jesus, I can talk, I fly everywhere.

Beat.

ESTHER. I stopped off on my way back home. I don't know why. Couldn't face what was back there I guess. The empty rooms. There was a nice church that caught my eye but when I stopped it was locked –

CHRIS. Sounds symbolic.

ESTHER. so I ended up in here.

CHRIS. From belief to processed beef.

ESTHER. Sorry?

CHRIS. Ignore me.

Beat.

ESTHER. My dad turned up.

CHRIS. What do you mean?

ESTHER. He's like one of those insects that incubate underground for years and then appear every decade or something. Only in his case it's every other year.

CHRIS. When did he turn up?

ESTHER. Last night. He wants me to look after him like I used to.

CHRIS. When was that?

ESTHER. He says he's struggling.

CHRIS. Tell him no.

ESTHER. He showed me this video, this police video on Facebook, when they arrested Rachel's guy –

CHRIS. Tell him he shouldn't watch that stuff.

ESTHER. he's in this room, some police room, crying. Like he's the sort who fucking cries, that's what my dad said. It made him so angry.

CHRIS. It's morbid.

ESTHER. My dad was always so full of rage.

CHRIS. Hold on.

ESTHER. What is it?

CHRIS. I thought they called my flight.

ESTHER. Did they?

CHRIS. Soon.

ESTHER. Why he turned up now I don't know. It's like he sensed something. I don't know what he wants from me. He's the sort that will spout on about morals – or whatever – but never apply it to themselves. He hurt us so much. As kids. Emotionally. He told me not to see Rachel's guy. I told him not to come back.

Beat.

CHRIS. Sounds difficult.

ESTHER. Sorry.

CHRIS. It's sad.

ESTHER. I've dumped a load of stuff on you.

CHRIS. I have been told I'm a good listener.

ESTHER. Well, thank you.

CHRIS. It's something I've practised.

ESTHER. Practised?

CHRIS. Does that sound weird?

ESTHER. It's good to develop yourself.

CHRIS. I try anyway.

ESTHER. It's good.

CHRIS. I was always someone who rushes around, always thinking ahead, not staying in the conversation. That's who I was. But now I practise listening more and it works for me. Mindfulness. I tell you it was a difficult change but that's the benefit of therapy.

ESTHER. Jesus, does everyone do therapy these days?

CHRIS. Oh, listen, if I had kids – not that I'm saying I want kids –

ESTHER. No –

CHRIS. not that I have anything against them in principle –

ESTHER. It's okay –

CHRIS. I would tell them, train to be a therapist –

ESTHER. There'll always be a need.

CHRIS. That or a lawyer.

Beat.

ESTHER. Chris –

CHRIS. Hold on –

ESTHER. Yes?

CHRIS. Gate thirteen.

ESTHER. Do you want to keep going?

CHRIS. Yes, I need to go soon.

ESTHER. Do you want to keep going with us?

CHRIS. Oh – sorry – I misheard you.

ESTHER. We never see each other –

CHRIS. Do you want to keep going?

ESTHER. we struggle to find time to talk –

CHRIS. I did try earlier.

ESTHER. don't you think?

CHRIS. No.

ESTHER. No?

CHRIS. It's just a difficult time.

ESTHER. Is it?

CHRIS. You're busy.

ESTHER. You're away a lot.

CHRIS. Autumn is academic hell.

ESTHER. Yes.

CHRIS. What I'm saying is –

ESTHER. Yes?

CHRIS. absolutely.

ESTHER. You want us to carry on?

CHRIS. Yes, I do. Look I've been on a good few dates this year –

ESTHER. I have too –

CHRIS. and you know what it's like – you know? – you have to grab the quality when you see it in this game – and you are quality, Esther, a one-off, believe me. There's something about you. So – yes – I want us to carry on.

Beat.

I should have made my feelings clear on that.

ESTHER. Okay.

CHRIS. Okay.

ESTHER. Things feel a little dark over here at the moment for me, so I just wanted to make sure this is going somewhere, you know? – that we have the potential at least – I had a sense you were looking for the same. You're looking to leave stuff behind too. That's my goal anyway.

CHRIS. Absolutely. We can absolutely agree on that. I don't want to be the guy I am now. I'm pretty sure about that.

Beat.

ESTHER. You should get your flight.

CHRIS. Yes.

ESTHER. Where are you going?

CHRIS. Stockholm.

ESTHER. Can you get duty-free there?

CHRIS. What do you want?

ESTHER. Marlboro Red.

CHRIS. I didn't know you smoked.

ESTHER. You don't have to.

CHRIS. Well, tobacco production is nearly as bad as beef.

Beat.

ESTHER. Stockholm sounds cold.

CHRIS. I think the weather is much like here.

ESTHER. Where's here?

CHRIS. The airport.

ESTHER. I know you are at the airport.

CHRIS. Sorry.

ESTHER. Which one?

CHRIS. Luton.

ESTHER. Luton?

CHRIS. Yeah, it's difficult finding flights to Stockholm at this time of the day and all I could get was some budget flight from Luton.

ESTHER. But why are you in Luton?

CHRIS. I just said.

ESTHER. Have you been in London?

CHRIS. Oh –

ESTHER. Where in London were you?

CHRIS. I had a meeting at King's.

ESTHER. Is that central?

CHRIS. It was a last-minute thing.

ESTHER. We could have met.

CHRIS. Did the meeting and then Tate Modern and then off.

ESTHER. You went to the Tate?

CHRIS. It's my mum. She's a member and we usually meet there once a month. I've been away a lot so I felt bad.

ESTHER. Your mum?

CHRIS. It was good to reconnect with the real core things.

ESTHER. I don't understand –

CHRIS. I'm sorry –

ESTHER. I don't understand –

CHRIS. I should have said –

ESTHER. what am I doing –

CHRIS. I'm –

ESTHER. with –

CHRIS. sorry.

ESTHER. this?

CHRIS. Esther?

ESTHER. This is confusing, Chris.

CHRIS. Esther?

ESTHER. I'm just confused by this now.

11.

Evening.

ESTHER *sits on the floor.*

She's holding a picture of Rachel cut from the newspaper.

She takes out a packet of cigarettes – quickly this time – and lights one.

12.

Day.

KEITH *sits*.

ESTHER *arrives*.

KEITH. Alright?

ESTHER. Hi.

KEITH. What's up?

ESTHER. I'm okay.

KEITH. You're definitely not okay.

ESTHER. Getting into here can be a bit of an ordeal, that's all.

KEITH. What?

ESTHER. That guard –

KEITH. Which one?

ESTHER. The one before coming into this room.

KEITH. What about him?

ESTHER. He always says something.

KEITH. What's he say?

ESTHER. I don't want to –

KEITH. What's he say?

ESTHER. Something about being your groupie.

KEITH. What?

ESTHER. That's what it sounded like.

KEITH. The fucker.

ESTHER. I'm fine.

KEITH. I'll have a word.

ESTHER. No.

KEITH. I'll have a word with him.

ESTHER. I said no.

Beat.

KEITH. It's good to have someone to look after you around here.

Beat.

ESTHER. I got you these.

She gets out a carton of Marlboro cigarettes but with one pack missing.

KEITH. Thanks.

ESTHER. That's okay.

KEITH. There's one missing.

ESTHER. I kept one back.

KEITH. Who for?

ESTHER. Me.

KEITH. What, you smoking again?

Pause.

Autumn. Isn't it? The weather.

ESTHER. Is it?

Beat.

KEITH. You don't like autumn. You said before.

Pause.

My mum came to see me.

ESTHER. How was that?

KEITH. She wittered on.

ESTHER. About what?

KEITH. I mean, after not seeing your son for a year you'd expect her to have something to say.

ESTHER. She's confused.

KEITH. Yeah, well –

Beat.

I don't know what she wants, I don't know what she wants
from me. She sits there and goes on and on about how I was
some beautiful baby. I mean all babies look the same, don't
they? As if what a baby looks like is any sign of anything.

Beat.

She does this pause thing after she says stuff like she's
expecting me to tell her something, answer something. Am
I supposed to have the answer? I don't have answers. I don't
have any fucking answers. It's like I say to the shrink in here,
it's you who should have the answers. You tell me the
answer. You tell me who I am. You tell me what you think
and do us all a favour.

Beat.

I don't want you to see her.

ESTHER. Me?

KEITH. Just come to see me.

ESTHER. Why?

KEITH. It's disturbing her.

ESTHER. She seems to like it.

KEITH. No.

ESTHER. I like it.

KEITH. If you're trying to get to me, don't bother her.

ESTHER. I'm not trying to get to you.

KEITH. No?

ESTHER. No.

KEITH. I told her not to come again.

Beat.

I tell you something, where I'm from there's only one reason to check on a guy's mum.

ESTHER. That's not why I went to see her.

KEITH. Do you know what I'm talking about?

ESTHER. I'm seeing someone.

Beat.

KEITH. You have a boyfriend?

ESTHER. I'm seeing this guy –

KEITH. Who is he?

ESTHER. Chris.

KEITH. You're seeing him?

ESTHER. Yes.

Beat.

KEITH. I didn't know you had a boyfriend.

ESTHER. He's not my boyfriend.

KEITH. What is he then?

ESTHER. He wasn't happy I come here.

KEITH. I bet he wasn't.

ESTHER. Not that he says that exactly.

KEITH. What has he said then?

ESTHER. He thinks it's weird –

KEITH. What's weird?

ESTHER. visiting my sister's murderer.

Beat.

KEITH. I suppose that would be weird.

ESTHER. If you are her murderer.

Beat.

KEITH. It didn't stop you coming though.

ESTHER. He's away.

KEITH. Where?

ESTHER. When we Skype the room always looks the same.

KEITH. Tell me about it.

Beat.

You must see more of me than you do of him then.

ESTHER. Not really.

KEITH. In the flesh, I mean.

Beat.

It's good you ignored him.

ESTHER. I didn't ignore him.

KEITH. Because I've been waiting for you –

Beat.

thinking about – how –

Beat.

you – look like –

Beat.

ESTHER. You said you didn't know her.

KEITH. What?

ESTHER. You said you didn't know my sister.

KEITH. When did I say that?

ESTHER. And now you say I remind you of her.

KEITH. Your sister? No.

Beat.

What?

Beat.

ESTHER. How do I remind you of her?

KEITH. What's this boyfriend of yours do?

ESTHER. He's not my boyfriend.

KEITH. Oh.

ESTHER. We're just dating.

KEITH. Dating.

ESTHER. We'll see how it goes.

KEITH. Fucking him yet?

> *Beat.*

> Don't mind me. It gets a bit frustrating in here.

> *Beat.*

ESTHER. Tell me how I remind you of her.

KEITH. I was just guessing –

ESTHER. Guessing?

KEITH. how you might be similar –

ESTHER. What's your guess?

KEITH. from the newspaper pictures.

ESTHER. Go on.

KEITH. Nah.

> *Beat.*

> Your throat.

ESTHER. My throat?

KEITH. Yeah.

> *Pause.*

> I'm just guessing, right? Your throat. Your neck. Hair. I like
> dark hair. Sisters have the same hair, don't they? Your
> mouth. It's kind of downwards at the edge like you're always

sad about something. I bet it's like that when you laugh as well. It's that kind of mouth.

Beat.

I could kiss that mouth.

Beat.

That throat.

Pause.

ESTHER. Did you kiss her mouth?

KEITH. I didn't know her.

ESTHER. If you had met her, would you have kissed her mouth.

KEITH. If she looked like you.

ESTHER. She did.

KEITH. Absolutely.

ESTHER. Would you have kissed her neck?

KEITH. Yeah.

ESTHER. Her throat?

KEITH. Especially her throat.

ESTHER. She would have let you?

KEITH. She wanted it too.

ESTHER. Did she?

KEITH. Yeah.

ESTHER. She told you that?

KEITH. No.

ESTHER. So how did you know?

KEITH. I could just tell.

ESTHER. Could you?

KEITH. Yeah.

ESTHER. How?

KEITH. Oh, come on.

ESTHER. Tell me.

KEITH. She was wet.

Beat.

That's a joke.

Pause.

Come closer.

ESTHER. No.

KEITH. I want to ask you something.

Beat.

Tell me how?

ESTHER. How what?

KEITH. When you saw me in the court you knew I had done it.

ESTHER. Yes.

KEITH. The first time you came here you said that.

ESTHER. Yes.

KEITH. How did you know?

ESTHER. I don't know.

KEITH. It was how I looked?

ESTHER. No.

KEITH. What then?

ESTHER. I sensed something.

KEITH. Sensed?

ESTHER. Yes.

KEITH. What sense?

ESTHER. I don't know.

KEITH. Smell.

ESTHER. No.

KEITH. You didn't touch me.

ESTHER. I wouldn't touch you.

KEITH. No?

ESTHER. No.

KEITH. You couldn't taste me.

ESTHER. I wouldn't –

KEITH. My accent?

ESTHER. I felt it.

KEITH. You felt you knew me?

ESTHER. I'm right, aren't I?

KEITH. I know why you are here even if you do have
    a boyfriend.

Pause.

ESTHER. I didn't say I don't like autumn. It's spiders. When
    spiders come inside. Making their webs. That's what I don't
    like.

Beat.

KEITH. No one judges spiders, do they? They just look at them
    and accept them. People might be scared, not like them,
    whatever, but no one thinks they should be something else.
    Like spiders should be pink butterflies. Everyone knows
    a spider is a spider and people might not like the thought that
    a spider exists and does what it does, I mean a spider does
    gruesome things, right? People don't think it's bad, they just
    think the spider is born that way and does what it was born
    to do whether they like it or not.

Beat.

You know in this world there have to be spiders as well as there have to be flies. I can see you know that.

Beat.

Don't go to my mum's again.

Beat.

Yeah?

13.

Evening.

ESTHER *stands waiting, nervous.*

As time passes her breathing becomes more and more uncontrolled.

She paces and finishes on her hands and knees, struggling for breath.

Eventually and with great effort she manages to regain control.

She remains sitting, still.

14.

Night.

ESTHER *and* CHRIS *stand apart.*

ESTHER. Hi.

CHRIS. Hey.

ESTHER. How's the hotel?

CHRIS. Way cooler than in Stockholm.

ESTHER. I thought you were in Stockholm.

CHRIS. Berlin.

ESTHER. You're in Berlin?

CHRIS. Well, I hope this is Berlin.

ESTHER. The room looks like all the others.

CHRIS. No, it's boutique.

ESTHER. Is it?

CHRIS. Black lampshades – look – black bedspread.

ESTHER. Thanks for calling.

CHRIS. Ah, you broke up there.

ESTHER. Sorry I missed your call earlier.

CHRIS. Say that again.

ESTHER. I got your message.

CHRIS. Are you at home?

ESTHER. It's late.

CHRIS. Some guys from the conference wanted to go for
a beer.

Beat.

Look – about the last time –

ESTHER. It's okay –

CHRIS. It was not okay –

ESTHER. it's forgotten already.

CHRIS. I tried to explain in Messenger.

ESTHER. I get it, your mum is important. It's – sweet.

CHRIS. Jesus, no.

ESTHER. I get that sometimes it's only family that helps.

CHRIS. But – sweet?

ESTHER. Sweet is good in my book.

CHRIS. Is it?

ESTHER. And mums are important.

CHRIS. I did try to touch base with you earlier.

ESTHER. Yes, I got your message.

CHRIS. Were you busy today?

ESTHER. I was out.

CHRIS. I wanted to talk about this sooner.

ESTHER. Well, we're talking now.

CHRIS. Yes.

ESTHER. So I consider my base touched.

CHRIS. Do you?

ESTHER. Yeah.

Beat.

How long have we known each other now, Chris?

CHRIS. Known each other?

ESTHER. I bet when you looked at my profile picture you –

CHRIS. What?

ESTHER. I bet you thought she looks uncomplicated.

CHRIS. You looked great in your picture. You look great now.

ESTHER. Despite my mouth going down at the edges even when I laugh.

CHRIS. What's that mean?

ESTHER. Did you notice that?

CHRIS. I don't know what that means.

ESTHER. Can I try something with you, Chris?

CHRIS. Sure.

Beat.

ESTHER. Have you ever had Skype sex?

CHRIS. What?

ESTHER. Have you?

CHRIS. Are you really asking me that?

ESTHER. Is that a no?

CHRIS. Yes, I mean no.

ESTHER. No, me neither.

CHRIS. That's what you want to try?

ESTHER. It might help – I don't know – reset us.

CHRIS. Sounds – yeah.

ESTHER. It might be fun, you know.

CHRIS. I'm up for new things.

ESTHER. Yeah – it's just for fun.

CHRIS. Some light knockabout.

ESTHER. Only if you want to.

Beat.

CHRIS. Okay.

ESTHER. Okay?

CHRIS. Let's do Skype sex.

ESTHER. Okay.

CHRIS. Can we use another phrase?

ESTHER. Like what?

CHRIS. Cybersex.

ESTHER. Is that better?

CHRIS. Probably not.

ESTHER. No.

Beat.

CHRIS. Okay.

ESTHER. Yes.

CHRIS. How does it work exactly?

ESTHER. How do you think it works?

CHRIS. We could start by speaking stuff out loud.

ESTHER. Well, I'm not jumping into a solo on-screen performance for you.

CHRIS. Oh, God, no – that would be exploitative.

Beat.

Okay.

ESTHER. Okay.

CHRIS. I'll start.

ESTHER. Okay.

CHRIS. What are you wearing?

ESTHER. What am I wearing?

CHRIS. Isn't that how this starts?

ESTHER. No.

CHRIS. Why's that so funny?

ESTHER. You can see what I'm wearing.

CHRIS. I saw some film and that's how they started.

ESTHER. Yes, when it's done on the telephone.

CHRIS. I am joking.

ESTHER. Just describe things.

Beat.

CHRIS. I gently place my hand on your left breast.

ESTHER. Hey, slow down.

CHRIS. What?

ESTHER. Let's go back a few steps.

CHRIS. Yes.

ESTHER. Okay, then.

CHRIS. I run my fingers through your hair.

ESTHER. That's better.

CHRIS. I kiss you gently on the mouth.

ESTHER. Yes.

CHRIS. I bite your lip.

ESTHER. Yes.

CHRIS. Gently.

ESTHER. You do.

CHRIS. Is this right?

ESTHER. Yes.

CHRIS. I pull you close.

ESTHER. Yes.

CHRIS. Pull you tight to me.

ESTHER. Yes.

CHRIS. Kiss your forehead.

ESTHER. Yes.

CHRIS. Kiss your jawline.

ESTHER. My throat.

CHRIS. Kiss your neck.

ESTHER. Yeah.

CHRIS. Just below the ear, your shoulder.

ESTHER. My throat.

CHRIS. Kiss your throat.

ESTHER. Yes.

CHRIS. Your chin.

ESTHER. Your hand caresses my face.

CHRIS. Yes.

ESTHER. My neck.

CHRIS. Our bodies are pressed hard together.

ESTHER. My throat.

CHRIS. We breathe together.

ESTHER. Your hand tightens.

CHRIS. Okay.

ESTHER. Gently.

CHRIS. It tightens?

ESTHER. Gently tightens on my throat.

CHRIS. My hand?

ESTHER. Just gently.

CHRIS. I'm not comfortable with this.

ESTHER. Are you stopping?

CHRIS. No, but –

ESTHER. You kiss me harder.

CHRIS. Okay –

ESTHER. Really hard.

CHRIS. I'm stopping.

ESTHER. Why?

CHRIS. I don't know –

ESTHER. What?

CHRIS. I don't feel –

ESTHER. What is it?

CHRIS. It doesn't feel –

ESTHER. So you're stopping?

CHRIS. It doesn't feel right.

   Beat.

ESTHER. No, you're right.

CHRIS. I'm sorry.

ESTHER. This was such a stupid idea –

CHRIS. No.

ESTHER. I wanted to try something out –

CHRIS. No.

ESTHER. I wanted to feel –

CHRIS. It's not the cybersex.

ESTHER. I wanted to get close to her –

CHRIS. it's –

ESTHER. I wanted –

CHRIS. it's just –

ESTHER. I want to understand.

CHRIS. didn't that guy –

ESTHER. Yes.

CHRIS. it jumped into my head –

ESTHER. Yes. He did.

CHRIS. your sister –

ESTHER. Oh, God, you're looking at me –

CHRIS. no –

ESTHER. you think I'm some sort of nutcase –

CHRIS. no –

ESTHER. don't you?

CHRIS. maybe –

ESTHER. You do.

CHRIS. no – maybe it's a delayed-shock thing –

ESTHER. Shock?

CHRIS. shock makes you do things out of character.

ESTHER. Out of character?

CHRIS. Yes –

ESTHER. No –

CHRIS. don't you think?

ESTHER. this is in character –

CHRIS. Esther –

ESTHER. yes, this is totally in character –

CHRIS. Esther –

ESTHER. this is who I am really.

CHRIS. Jesus.

ESTHER. Why are you looking at me like that?

CHRIS. Like what?

ESTHER. Don't look at me like that, Chris.

CHRIS. I'm not –

ESTHER. I can't let you look at me like that.

CHRIS. Have you been to see him again?

ESTHER. Who?

CHRIS. The guy – the guy – the fucking guy who is so obviously fucking you up –

ESTHER. He's not fucking me up.

CHRIS. your sister's fucking guy.

ESTHER. Yes – I saw him again.

CHRIS. Fucking hell, Esther –

ESTHER. Don't –

CHRIS. fucking hell.

ESTHER. no, Chris –

CHRIS. Really?

ESTHER. I have to see him –

CHRIS. You don't.

ESTHER. Yes, I do – you have to take that or leave it.

15.

Evening.

ESTHER *is on the floor.*

Beat.

ESTHER. Yes – yes – I'm okay –

> *Beat.*
>
> Honestly – I just – sometimes – it all comes flooding back but it's okay.
>
> *She takes a deep, controlled breath.*
>
> I'm better now – so –
>
> *Beat.*
>
> I know, I know – I know what's what – okay?
>
> *Beat.*
>
> Thanks for checking, though, Rachel.
>
> *She takes out a cigarette and looks at it.*
>
> *She decides not to light it.*

16.

Late afternoon.

CHRIS *and* ESTHER *stand separately.*

ESTHER*'s phone rings and she looks at it.*

She pushes it to voicemail.

CHRIS. Hi. It's me, Chris. I'm sorry I haven't been in touch –
I'm away – no excuse but I'm in Amsterdam – working –
going to the galleries. Mondrian today with his lines, over
and over. That's his thing. You should check him out. I like
him. It's weird but – actually I'm pulled to the same stuff all
the time, you know – I was thinking exactly this today – you
know how I used to say that there are no patterns, there is
nothing in fact, in my 'speech', remember? – but today
I thought actually we like seeing the same patterns, all of us,
don't we? – I really think we do and it's hard – I guess – to
change that and hard to fit yourself into someone else's –
Jesus – sorry.

Beat.

Let me start again. Sorry. I want to get this right. I'm being
a bit abstract.

ESTHER *puts her phone away.*

I've thought a lot about us waiting at the airports and I'm not
sure it's working – with us. We kind of ended up somewhere
we didn't expect – well, I did. I'm still working on things –
like you are – I know you are too – and – well, I guess it's
unfair on you if I get too fixed on anything or anyone before
I've sorted my stuff out, you know, and I'm not sure how
long that will take – so I don't want you to feel you have to
wait around – look, I'm waffling on, I don't want to clog up
your voicemail. Good luck with everything. I hope you find
the one that means you can delete the app. That's what we're
all looking for – I guess.

17.

Day.

KEITH *and* ESTHER *sit facing each other.*

Pause.

KEITH. Everything okay?

ESTHER. Before I forget –

KEITH. Yeah?

ESTHER. let me give you these.

    She hands him a packet of Marlboro cigarettes from her bag.

KEITH. What's that?

ESTHER. It's the missing pack.

KEITH. What?

ESTHER. It's a terrible habit.

KEITH. Have them.

ESTHER. I don't want to smoke.

    Pause.

KEITH. Are you alright?

ESTHER. Yes.

KEITH. You seem – somehow –

    Beat.

    There's something wrong.

ESTHER. No.

KEITH. I thought I frightened you off.

ESTHER. No.

KEITH. It's what I've been mulling on.

ESTHER. I wasn't frightened.

KEITH. That's what I thought.

ESTHER. So there's no need to apologise.

KEITH. I wasn't apologising.

Beat.

I'm glad you came back.

Beat.

How's your boyfriend?

ESTHER. He wasn't my boyfriend.

KEITH. Wasn't?

ESTHER. That's right.

Beat.

KEITH. So, it's over?

ESTHER. He didn't turn out to be the person I thought he was.

Beat.

KEITH. Okay – well – probably for the best.

ESTHER. Yes.

KEITH. He'd have stopped you coming in the end.

ESTHER. He would never have stopped me.

KEITH. You wanted to keep coming?

ESTHER. Yes.

KEITH. Well, that's good to know.

Beat.

ESTHER. Actually, that's what I've been trying to understand.

KEITH. Yeah?

ESTHER. Why I did keep coming back.

KEITH. And what have you come up with?

Beat.

ESTHER. I wanted to forgive you – at first – it's what we were taught, it felt like respecting what I was but then – you asked me to come back and I did, more than once, I was pulled – for a while – and I thought there was something wrong with me – really – I was driving here and back, driving for miles and – I thought there must be something wrong with me deep inside – and I thought – I thought, was there something wrong with her too?

KEITH. Right.

ESTHER. Maybe there's something about our family.

KEITH. Maybe –

ESTHER. I stared at her photo to see if she was drawn to you –

KEITH. maybe there is.

ESTHER. drawn to men like you –

KEITH. Like me?

ESTHER. perhaps you had something she wanted –

KEITH. I never met her –

ESTHER. because of what Dad did to us –

KEITH. I never met her –

ESTHER. after my mum left –

Beat.

and maybe I was the same.

Beat.

That's what I thought.

KEITH. All of that's got nothing to do with me.

Beat.

ESTHER. I went to see your mum again.

Beat.

KEITH. What's got into you today?

ESTHER. She asked me to.

KEITH. I told you not to see her any more.

ESTHER. I know.

KEITH. That's totally pissed me off to be honest.

ESTHER. I know how she felt.

KEITH. Yeah – well – fucking – my mum? If she was a real mum, she would know what I'm really like, what I am on the inside – but that's not what she is. Someone is always breaking her heart by telling her some home truth she's ignored. She can't blame me for that. She should break a habit of a lifetime and take a good look at things. I've never been a saint. Did you tell her to write to me?

ESTHER. She said she might.

KEITH. You've got to stop seeing her.

ESTHER. She –

KEITH. Did you fucking hear me?

Beat.

Let me tell you what pisses me off about you seeing her – I said not to – we had an understanding – there was something between us, wasn't there?

ESTHER. No.

KEITH. The first time you came here, it was there – a connection – you told me. The last time you came we talked and I knew I had you –

ESTHER. You didn't have me.

KEITH. You felt the same.

ESTHER. No.

KEITH. Like – love –

ESTHER. Love?

KEITH. It happens.

ESTHER. No.

KEITH. The guy next door married his penpal.

ESTHER. No.

KEITH. The cigarettes.

ESTHER. I wasn't in love.

KEITH. Who was then? Me?

> *Beat.*

> Fuck.

> *Beat.*

> Whatever it was – you're really fucking ruining it now.

ESTHER. Your mum told me she had seen Rachel.

> *Beat.*

KEITH. She what?

ESTHER. She saw Rachel.

> *Beat.*

> She saw my sister.

KEITH. For fuck's sake.

> *Beat.*

> When?

ESTHER. She was in your taxi.

KEITH. No.

ESTHER. Outside your mum's house.

KEITH. No.

ESTHER. On the evening Rachel died.

KEITH. No.

ESTHER. You said you didn't know Rachel.

Beat.

KEITH. Why didn't she tell the police then?

ESTHER. She didn't want to.

KEITH. It's bullshit.

Beat.

She's full of shit.

ESTHER. She didn't want to lose you.

KEITH. Bollocks.

ESTHER. Her picture of you.

KEITH. Stop fucking with me here.

ESTHER. Did you kill my sister?

Beat.

Did you kill Rachel?

Beat.

Tell me.

Beat.

Tell me what happened.

Beat.

I need to know.

Pause.

Okay, I'll go then, shall I?

KEITH. Go?

ESTHER. Yes.

KEITH. Why would you go?

ESTHER. There's nothing for me here.

KEITH. What's got into you today? First I thought we had some
kind of connection and then it turns out no – fucking hard to
believe to be honest – then banging on about my mum – fuck
my mum, yeah? – now you're going? After all we've been
through together. It's bullshit.

ESTHER *stands*.

Okay.

Beat.

Sit down.

Beat.

She sits.

Pause.

Yes.

ESTHER. What?

KEITH. Yes.

ESTHER. Why?

KEITH. I don't know.

ESTHER. You don't know?

KEITH. No.

ESTHER. Jesus.

KEITH. Things just went that way.

ESTHER. Jesus.

KEITH. It just went that way.

ESTHER. Jesus.

KEITH. Let me explain.

ESTHER. Jesus.

KEITH. I picked her up – in the West End – she said she been
   doing happy hour – after work – she looked great – her hair –
   sexy but not – and it was like a sign, an omen – she wanted to
   go east – she wanted to go my way – and she was a bit drunk
   and she laughed – I had tried a few gags, you know, to warm
   up the atmosphere and – and – the laughter was so good – this
   drive with us just talking and laughing – I said that we are like
   neighbours – I'll show you the sights, my mum's house, where
   I grew up, I'll show you the manger – and she laughed and she
   said, 'sure, Jesus' – which made me laugh, 'I need to go
   home', she said she was tired – so I showed her where I grew
   up and she laughed again – she – and I looked at it – and – that
   shitty house – that shitty house – I looked and – how shit it
   looked – and how classy she was – she had seen that – she had
   seen the shit – she had seen how shit I was and she had
   laughed – and – it was wrong – she had felt so different, she
   had made me feel so different – but she laughed – and I –
   I couldn't let her – I couldn't let – she said she wanted to go
   now, she wanted to go home but – but – no – why did she have
   to laugh? And then I knew that I had to do it.

ESTHER. Stop it –

KEITH. I kept thinking this was wrong –

ESTHER. Stop it –

KEITH. but I couldn't – stop –

ESTHER. Stop it –

KEITH. and then I couldn't –

ESTHER. No –

KEITH. admit it –

ESTHER. No –

KEITH. even to myself –

ESTHER. You could have stopped.

KEITH. I kept thinking I should never have done Rachel –

ESTHER. But you did.

KEITH. Yes –

ESTHER. You did.

KEITH. but –

ESTHER. What?

KEITH. now I know what I am.

ESTHER. You know what you are?

KEITH. It was all leading to this. That's what therapy told me.

She stands.

ESTHER. What you did to us – did you never realise?

KEITH. What are you doing?

She sits.

ESTHER. You hurt her, you hurt us when you didn't admit it, you dragged us through it all again and again and again – the trial, the cruelty of it, the sheer arrogance, you pleaded innocent and it disgusts me. You disgust me.

KEITH. Listen to me –

ESTHER. It had nothing to do with her, her laugh, it wasn't her laugh – her laugh was – no, it wasn't her, it wasn't us, it was you, you did it –

KEITH. but I couldn't help it –

ESTHER. No – no – oh Jesus – what, because you're a spider? Is that it? Is it?

KEITH. no – listen –

ESTHER. You're a man – all hate, self-pity, ego and angry – I felt pity sitting with you –

KEITH. Pity?

ESTHER. you're nothing – you're nothing – to me, you've always been nothing.

She stands again.

KEITH. You can't leave.

ESTHER. Yes. Now I can go.

She leaves.

KEITH. Come back here. What? No fucking way. I'm not having that – fucking pity me and leave? Leave me. Fuck that. Bitch. Fuck you. Fuck you. You don't get to do that. Get fucking back here.

A bell rings.

18.

Evening.

ESTHER *stands.*

Silence.

ESTHER. I've got a confession. I don't feel quite ready. I've been running things over. Sorting a few things out, I guess. Pumping myself up.

Beat.

Jesus – I'm so stupid – I've come this far I should just keep going – what time is it, Rachel? Oh –

Beat.

Okay – okay –

Beat.

So – I'm going to walk out there and I'm going to do it. I'm going to walk up to her – say hello – and talk first. I'll say, if I had held on to what I felt was me too tightly over the past year I would have ended up in a very dark place. I've learnt to hold on to what I needed and I made up the rest. Which will make me sound like a weirdo but it'll be okay. I'll say that's why I'm here. That's what I learnt. It's true. I let go.

Beat.

No – I can't say that –

Beat.

I'll say smiling changes your brain. Try it. Two minutes of your time, what have you got to lose? That's all it takes to change your brain. Change you. Let's do it together. Change both of us. That's it. Yeah. I know it feels weird but just keep going. Two minutes.

ESTHER *keeps smiling, warmly.*

That's it, keep smiling.

Beat.

I'll say, keep smiling, Mum –

Beat.

let's keep smiling –

Beat.

together –

Beat.

and she does –

Beat.

she smiles –

Beat.

we both smile –

Beat.

and we both feel different –

ESTHER *is smiling.*

we both feel like new.

ESTHER *continues to smile as the light disappears.*

A Nick Hern Book

Spiderfly first published in Great Britain in 2019 as a paperback original by Nick Hern Books Limited, The Glasshouse, 49a Goldhawk Road, London W12 8QP, in association with Metal Rabbit and Theatre503

Spiderfly copyright © 2019 John Webber

John Webber has asserted his moral right to be identified as the author of this work

Designed and typeset by Nick Hern Books, London
Printed in Great Britain by Mimeo Ltd, Huntingdon, Cambridgeshire PE29 6XX

A CIP catalogue record for this book is available from the British Library

ISBN   978 1 84842 904 8

Woodland
CARBON
www.woodlandcarbon.co.uk
NICK HERN BOOKS
Printed on Carbon Captured paper

www.nickhernbooks.co.uk

facebook.com/nickhernbooks

twitter.com/nickhernbooks